BEACONS
of
HOPE

SANDRA DORSAINVIL

BEACONS of HOPE

XULON PRESS

Xulon Press
2301 Lucien Way #415
Maitland, FL 32751
407.339.4217
www.xulonpress.com

Editor: Kathryn Anastasia. Retired educator, mentor and advocate for first generation students for 45 years. She volunteers with the St. Vincent de Paul Society at a local food pantry in the Boston area. She is a member of the Board at Bethany Hill Place in Massachusetts.

Paperback ISBN-13: 978-1-6628-3826-2
eBook ISBN-13: 978-1-6628-3827-9

Foreword

"L et your light so shine before men, that they may see your good works, and glorify your Father which is in heaven." Matthew 5: 16.KJV. The lives of many arriving to land from water depended on the men and women who managed the lighthouses dotting the coast of New England and even as far as Mississippi. They made sure that the light shone brightly night after night so others could safely navigate home. Working alongside husbands, fathers, or alone, a number of women occupied this important post. However, their voices, their lives, and their good work go unheard and unrecognized. In this devotional, Rev. Sandra Dorsainvil, urges the reader to contemplate the lives of these nameless women who made it their daily duty and obligation to ensure that the light shone brightly to guide others safely home. Rev. Dorsainvil takes us on a journey to learn more of these unsung women as well as helping us to explore how we grow the light we have been gifted from God to shine brightly in this dark and broken world.

"Neither do men light a candle, and put it under a bushel, but on a candlestick; and it giveth light unto all that are in the house." Matthew 5: 15.KJV. Most of the 15 women lighthouse keepers in this devotional,

despite faithfully tending to the lighthouses for more than two decades, remained nameless. They carried on the work alongside their husbands or fathers and beyond. They answered their call to shine the light night after night, carrying oil to light the lamps, so that others could safely navigate home. Just as these women answered their call and lived out their purpose, Rev. Dorsainvil encourages each of us over a 12-day period to examine and reflect daily on the lives of these faithful women. By doing so, we can prayerfully go deeper in discerning the light that God has placed in each of us. Everyone may not know your name, as was the case for many of these women, yet *"Fear not, for I have redeemed you; I have summoned you by name; you are mine."* Isaiah 43: 1.KJV

What is *your* name? Surely when you were born, your parents gave you a name by which family and friends use to call you. To others outside your immediate circle, you remain nameless, anonymous, or invisible. Despite this fact of anonymity, there is one who knows you by name. In many cultures around the world, naming a child has cultural or historical significance to the family or clan. The women portrayed in this devotional had a name given by their birth mother and father, yet our spiritual father, God, already knew their name and the purpose for their lives. I thank you Sandra, Sister in Christ, to invite all of us to journey with these bold and courageous women to discover the meaning of our name and to shine our light.

Susan C. Frazier-Kouassi, Ph.D., Director of the Texas Juvenile Crime Prevention Center, Prairie View A&M University; Prairie View, Texas & Founder/Executive Director of the Institute for Education of Women in Africa and the Diaspora (a 501(c)3 charitable non-profit organization)

Introduction

This 12-Day devotional seeks to shed light on 15 women lighthouse keepers in the United States, from the 19th and 20th century, who have gone unnoticed for many years before their official appointments were made by either a presidential appointment, by the US Coast Guard, or by the US Lighthouse Establishment. It is important to note that some of the women keepers started to work alongside their fathers or spouses long before any official appointment or salary. They were the ones climbing the staircases every night to fill the lamps with oil and keeping watch. They were unnoticed for many years or decades. All the women who were chosen for this devotional served for a minimum of twenty years of their lives. They worked on lighthouses in Connecticut, Florida, Louisiana, Maine, Maryland, Michigan, Mississippi, New York, and Rhode Island. Many had small children or younger siblings, and some had sick loved ones to also care for while attending to the daily functioning of the lighthouses. Many tended vegetable gardens and livestock while keeping a tidy home. All of them took pride in their work. These women's commitment was to save lives and provide light to dark shorelines. They upheld the second greatest Christian commandment Jesus proclaimed, found in all four gospels, which says "to love thy neighbour as thyself." When darkness fell, their hearts, hands, feet, and eyes formed a partnership with the lamps they filled every night. They became the beacons of hope for strangers at sea. The fact that little has been written about these women drew me to juxtapose some scripture passages of unnamed women of the Bible, taken from Proverbs to the book of Romans.

This 12-Day devotional is presented in a unique way. Each day, you are first introduced with some facts about a woman lighthouse keeper and her years and location of service, which is then followed by a short scripture reference of an unnamed woman of the Bible. The day concludes with some reflection questions. This inductive process is an invitation to enter into deeper dialogue with God. You will undoubtedly desire to know more about the women keepers, the lighthouses, and the scripture references. It will be good to have a dedicated blank book to capture your thoughts and journal with God, as you walk through these 12 days of devotion. It can be done in 12 days, 12 weeks, 12 months. The pace is spirit led. The chosen women for this devotional sacrificed their health, lives, and cultural status for strangers at sea. They upheld the love of life as they went up and down staircases, carrying oil, trimming wicks, which would light the way for a multitude. They lived *"and what doth the Lord require of thee, but to do justly, and to love mercy, and to walk humbly with thy God?"* Micah 6:8. KJV.

May you be inspired to find your voice of Hope as you read the following pages.

Sandra Dorsainvil

DAY #1 "Miss Abbie Burgess"
Dates of service: 1853 – 1872
Maine

Miss Abbie Burgess was born in 1839 on Matinicus Island where her father, Samuel Burgess, was appointed keeper of the Matinicus Rock Light Station in 1853. It is located 25 miles from the city of Rockland, the nearest port off the coast of Maine. Abbie was only 14 years old at the time of her father's appointment, when she started to assist her father with the lighthouse duties. On a couple of occasions, when Abbie's father had to sail to the mainland to fetch supplies, Abbie was left as the sole keeper of the lights. Due to political reasons, a new keeper was appointed in 1861 to the Matinicus Rock Light Station. His name was Captain John Grant, whom Abbie trained. Soon after she married Isaac Grant, who was Capt. John Grant's son, Abbie was appointed assistant keeper and started receiving a salary for her services. In 1869, a steam driven fog whistle was installed, due to severe weather conditions. In 1875, Isaac and Abbie Grant were appointed assistant keepers to Whitehead Light Station near Spruce Head in Maine. They served until 1890.

First Observations: What surprised you about her life?

Scripture to reflect on: Proverbs 31: 31 "Honor the women"
"Give her of the fruit of her hands; and let her own works praise her in the gates." KJV

The book of proverbs provides wise counsel for many life circumstances. Many chapters are attributed to King Solomon. Chapter 31 is attributed to King Lemuel. As we read this scripture and reflect on Abbie's life as a beacon of life for others around her, here are questions to help us with the intersection of scripture and her testimony. What does Abbie teach us?

Reflect: What might Proverbs 31 help convey to young girls searching for meaning in their lives? How does verse 31 inform how to best honor the work of your hands?

Act: How might choices made as a teenager inform choices to enter the threshold of adulthood in a justice minded way?

DAY #2 "Mrs. Zoradia Lewis & Mrs. Ida Lewis Wilson"
Dates of service: 1857 – 1911
Rhode Island

M rs. Zoradia Lewis and her daughter Miss Ida Lewis started attending to the daily duties of the Lime Rock Light Station in Newport Harbor, Rhode Island in 1857. Mr. Hosea Lewis suffered a debilitating stroke soon after the family had moved to the island in 1857. At age 15, Miss Ida Lewis, the eldest of four children, became the primary caretaker of her younger siblings, rowing them every day to shore, so they could attend school. At sundown and midnight the lamp would need to be filled with oil, the wick trimmed, and the reflectors polished, among other occasional repairs to the lighthouse. Miss Ida made daring sea rescues, when it was considered unladylike for a single woman to row boats. Mrs. Zoradia Lewis was appointed keeper of the lighthouse in 1872 after her husband's death. Her appointment lasted until 1879. Her daughter, now Mrs. Ida Lewis Wilson, was appointed keeper and received an annual salary until 1911, when she died. Before her death, Mrs. Ida Lewis Wilson was the first woman keeper to receive the Gold Lifesaving medal by the United States government for rescuing two soldiers from Fort Adams who had fallen through the ice.

Since 1924, the Rock Light Station has been renamed the Ida Lewis Rock lighthouse in honor of her life of dedication and heroic rescue efforts.

First Observations: What surprised you about their lives?

Scripture to reflect on: Acts 16: 13 "Women at prayer"
"And on the sabbath we went out of the city by a river side, where prayer was wont to be made; and we sat down, and spake unto the women which resorted thither." KJV

The Book of Acts, authored by the Evangelist Luke, speaks to the story of Christianity, the building of the Church, and the spread of the Gospel. In Acts 16, the Apostle Paul, a new convert to Christianity, is accompanied by Timothy, and they are traveling through the region of Phrygia, Galatia and heading to Macedonia. As we read this scripture and reflect on Ida's life, here are questions to help us with the intersection of scripture and her testimony. What does Ida teach us?

Reflect: How might Acts 16 help us to understand the power of communal prayer? What might God be asking of Christian leaders and educators to focus on as change agents?

Act: What character traits would you need to see in a servant leader in training?

DAY #3 "Mrs. Catherine Murdock"
Dates of service: 1857 – 1907
New York

Mrs. Catherine Murdock, pregnant with her third child, found herself managing all tasks at the Rondout Creek Light Station in New York, in 1857, a year after her husband's appointment. He died under tragic circumstances. Local friends were instrumental in Mrs. Catherine Murdock's official appointment after her husband's death. She stayed in the old weathered, damaged, wooden structure for ten years, steadfast in her duty of keeping the light to direct sailors on the proper course along the Hudson River. In 1867, a lighthouse built of stone was constructed on the south side of the creek entrance. The lantern was housed inside a granite tower on a round granite pier. The living quarters were sturdier and roomier than the old wooden structure Mrs. Catherine Murdock had known on the west side of the river. During the fifty years of service, Mrs. Catherine Murdock rescued and nursed many wounded seamen. She also attended to livestock. Mrs. Catherine Murdock retired from her post in 1907.

First Observations: What surprised you about her life?

Scripture to reflect on: Matthew 15: 21 – 28 "Canaanite Woman"
"Then Jesus went thence and departed into the coasts of Tyre and Sidon. And behold, a woman of Canaan came out of the same coasts, and cried unto him, saying," Have mercy on me, O Lord, thou son of David; my daughter is grievously vexed with a devil." But he answered her not a word. And his disciples came and besought him, saying, Send her away; for she crieth after us. But he answered and said, "I am not sent but unto the lost sheep of the house of Israel." Then came she and worshipped him, saying, "Lord, help me." But he answered and said, "It is not meet to take the children's bread, and to cast it to dogs." And she said, "Truth, Lord:

yet the dogs eat of the crumbs which fall from their masters' table." Then Jesus answered and said unto her " O woman, great is thy faith be it unto thee even as thou wilt." And her daughter was made whole from that very hour." KJV

In the Gospel of Matthew, we are shown that God's promises to Israel had been upheld, through the coming of Jesus, God's promised Messiah. The Apostle Matthew, born in Palestine, was a strong believer in the mission of Jesus. Even though he worked in Capernaum, Matthew found himself serving in the East, towards Persia.

As we read this scripture and reflect on Catherine's life, here are questions to help us with the intersection of scripture and her testimony. What does Catherine teach us?

Reflect: What cross-cultural stigmas were put aside as the Canaanite woman boldly approached Jesus? How can silence be a welcomed response from The Lord?

Act: How can you weave the intersection of joy, sadness, and grief during your faith walk?

DAY #4 "Miss Mary Reynolds, Mrs. Maria Younghans, Miss Miranda Younghans"
Dates of service: 1854 – 1929
Mississippi

H ere are some essential facts: the women who kept the nine lamps and fourteen-inch reflectors in working order at the Biloxi Light Station in Mississippi did so for a total of 74 years. It represents 81% of the years the lighthouse had appointed keepers. Miss Mary Reynolds received her appointment in 1854 because of advocacy efforts made by an elected local senator. She encountered political pressure to turn off the light during the Civil War. Mrs. Maria Younghans took over the duties after her husband passed away, less than a year after his appointment in 1867. She performed her duties until the age of 77 years old. These women climbed the stairs of the cast iron structure several times daily whether it was sunny or stormy outside. They repaired broken glasses among other tasks. A woman assistant keeper was appointed to Mrs. Maria Younghans in her later years of service. The same assistant continued when Miss Miranda (her daughter) assumed all the keeper's duties until she retired in 1929.

First Observation: What surprised you about their lives?

Scripture to reflect on: Mark 12: 41 – 44 "Widow's mite"
"And Jesus sat over against the treasury and beheld how the people cast money into the treasury: and many that were rich cast in much. And there came a certain poor widow, and she threw in two mites, which make a farthing. And he called unto him his disciples, and saith unto them, "Verily I say unto you, That this poor widow hath cast more in, than all they which have cast into the treasury: For all they did cast in of their abundance; but she of her want did cast in all that she had, even all her living." "KJV

The Gospel of Mark is believed to have been directed at a Gentile audience in Rome. It is the shortest Gospel and one to speak of Jesus' teachings and active ministry life with more reported miracles than in any other gospels. In this scripture passage, readers are presented with the status of widows, who were marginalized, in the cultural context of ancient Israel.

As we read this scripture and reflect on Mary's, Maria's, Miranda's and the unnamed assistant's lives, here are questions to help us with the intersection of scripture and their testimonies. What do Mary, Maria, Miranda, and the unnamed assistant teach us?

Reflect: What does Jesus' observation of the widow's generosity inform us about The Church? Has the tradition of tithing and giving changed as a form of worship?

Act: How might lessons on stewardship be presented using this scripture as a story of sacrificial giving and the women keepers?

DAY #5 "Miss Catherine Moore"
Dates of Service: 1817 – 1879
Connecticut

M iss Catherine "Kate" Moore was officially appointed keeper of the Black Rock Light Station located on the north shore of Long Island Sound, on Fayerweather Island off of Bridgeport, Connecticut, when she was 76 years old. She had been living at the keeper's home with her father, Stephen Tomlinson Moore, since 1817, when he was appointed keeper of the lighthouse. Miss Catherine Moore assisted her father, who had sustained physical injuries aboard a ship. He could not attend to the demanding nature of the work. Miss Catherine Moore took on caring for her father for 54 years while attending to the daily tasks of trimming eight wicks, carrying four gallons of whale oil each night up the tower, polishing off the reflectors to keep the brightness of the light constant, and making necessary repairs when needed. Besides these tasks, Miss Catherine Moore also tended to the livestock and garden, which she depended on for food. She frequently nursed to health sailors who were injured from boat accidents. She supplemented the income her father received from the US government, by harvesting oysters and selling handmade wood carvings to visitors. Miss Catherine Moore never received any formal education. She retired in 1879. She died at the age of 105 years old.

First Observation: What surprised you about her life?

Scripture to reflect on: Luke 13: 10 – 13 "Woman bent over"
"And he was teaching in one of the synagogues on the sabbath. And, behold, there was a woman which had a spirit of infirmity eighteen years, and was bowed together, and could in no wise lift up herself. And when Jesus saw her, he called her to him, and said unto her, "Woman, thou art loosed

from thine infirmity." And he laid his hands on her: and immediately she was made straight, and glorified God." KJV

In the gospel of Luke, the people of Israel were invited to follow Jesus whose ministry focused first in Galilee. The apostle Luke was known to have been a physician primarily preaching to the Gentiles. As we read this scripture and reflect on Catherine's life, here are questions to help us with the intersection of scripture and her testimony. What does Catherine teach us?

Reflect: How does Jesus address what others see as physical limitations?

How is God calling some to serve in His name anonymously?

Act: What attributes and character traits should be elevated in God's servants who work in the shadow of others?

DAY #6 "Mrs. Josephine Freeman"
Dates of service: 1876 – 1912
Maryland

Mrs. Josephine Freeman received the charge of keeping the oil burning at Blackistone Island Light Station on St Clements Island in Maryland from her father in 1875. Her brother had cared for the lighthouse before her from 1868 until 1875. St Clements Island was owned by her father.

Mrs. Josephine Freeman married a local farmer who gave up his farm to live at the lighthouse with her. He focused on hunting and fishing to provide food for his family. He brought his farming skills to the island. He did many building repairs when needed. They had four children who helped attend to some of the duties of maintaining good functioning of the lighthouse, especially at night. The Blackistone Island Light Station was referred to as Maryland's "Plymouth Rock." The lighthouse stood forty-six feet above the Potomac River. In 1856, a fourth-order Fresnel lens replaced the eleven oil lamps set in fourteen-inch reflectors. In 1888, a fog bell tower was built thirty feet from the main lighthouse building. Attending to the management and functioning of the Blackistone Island Light Station was a family endeavor.

Mrs. Josephine died in 1912 and her son William Freeman, Jr. continued the keeper's job. The lighthouse was automated in 1932, and fire destroyed it in 1956.

First Observations: What surprised you about her life?

Scripture to reflect on: Mark 5: 38 – 41 "Jairus' Daughter"
"And he cometh to the house of the ruler of the synagogue, and seeth the tumult, and them that wept and wailed greatly. And when he was come in,

he saith unto them, "Why make ye this ado, and weep? the damsel is not dead, but sleepeth." And they laughed him to scorn. But when he had put them all out, he taketh the father and the mother of the damsel, and them that were with him, and entereth in where the damsel was lying. And he took the damsel by the hand, and said unto her, "Talitha cumi;" which is, being interpreted, Damsel, I say unto thee," arise."" KJV

The Gospel of Mark is believed to have been directed at a Gentile audience in Rome. It is the shortest Gospel and one to speak of Jesus' teachings and active ministry life with more reported miracles than in any other gospels. In this scripture passage we see the intersection of crisis and hope, fear and despair, touching a family with means, considered to be part of a privileged social class in the cultural context in Capernaum. How is privilege perceived in Mrs. Josephine Freeman's life? As we read this scripture and reflect on Josephine's life, here are questions to help us with the intersection of scripture and her testimony. What does Josephine teach us?

<u>Reflect</u>: What traditions confront fear and despair in Jairus' eyes? What is Jesus teaching the disciples who have accompanied him?

<u>Act</u>: How do we overcome fear?

DAY #7 "Women Keepers Unofficially Appointed"
19th century
Maryland

Point Lookout Light Station in Scotland, Maryland, built in 1830 represents one of many lighthouses in the United States where women diligently attended to the daily duties of managing a lighthouse without any official appointments, salary, or recognition by the US Coast Guard, nor the Lighthouse establishments.

First Observations: Are you surprised to know that many women keepers were overlooked for decades?

Scripture to reflect on: Luke 8: 16 – 18
"No man, when he hath lighted a candle, covereth it with a vessel, or putteth it under a bed; but setteth it on a candlestick, that they which enter in may see the light. For nothing is secret, that shall not be made manifest; neither anything hid, that shall not be known and come abroad. Take heed therefore how ye hear: for whosoever hath, to him shall be given; and whosoever hath not, from him shall be taken even that which he seemeth to have." KJV

Reflect: What are some transforming stories, testimonies of God's omnipotence that need to be shared with new believers? How did the unnamed women appear in the sacred text?

Act: Who are the formative people in your faith journey, who need to be acknowledged?

DAY #8 "Mrs. Elizabeth Van Ripper Williams"
Dates of service: 1872 – 1913
Michigan

Mrs. Elizabeth Van Ripper Williams grew up on Beaver Island in Michigan, where she would become keeper of two lighthouses, the Beaver Island Harbor Point Light Station and the Little Traverse Light Station for 41 years, from 1872 until 1913. Mrs. Elizabeth Van Ripper Williams had been attending to the Beaver Island Harbor Point Light Station for a few years before she was appointed by the Lighthouse Board in 1872. Her husband's health was declining, and as she reports in her book, *A Child of the Sea; Life among the Mormons*, "My husband having now very poor health, I took charge of the care of the lamps, and the beautiful lens in the tower was my especial care....On stormy nights I watched the light that no accident might happen...In long nights the lamps had to be trimmed twice each night, and sometimes oftener." (Page 213)

Mrs. Elizabeth Van Ripper Williams managed all the duties at Beaver Island Harbor Point Light Station until 1884, when she requested to be transferred to the Little Traverse Light Station at Harbor Springs.

She was the first keeper at the newly built Little Traverse Light Station in 1884, which had a fog bell to attend to in addition to the lamps of the lighthouse. She kept her appointment for 29 years.

First Observations: What surprised you about her life?

Scripture to reflect on: Matthew 26: 69 – 72 "Two servant girls accuse Peter"
"Now Peter sat without in the palace: and a damsel came unto him, saying, "Thou also wast with Jesus of Galilee." But he denied before them all, saying,

*"I know not what thou sayest." And when he was gone out into the porch, another maid saw him, and said unto them that were there, "this fellow was also with Jesus of Nazareth." And again he denied with an oath," I do not know the man.""*KJV

In the Gospel of Matthew, we are shown that God's promises to Israel had been upheld, through the coming of Jesus, God's promised Messiah. The apostle Matthew, who was born in Palestine, was a strong believer in the mission of Jesus. His ministry took him to serve in the East, towards Persia, away from his comfort zone. He gave his heart and mind in service to The Lord. Mrs. Elizabeth Van Ripper Williams chose to serve in remote areas in Michigan.

As we read this scripture and reflect on Elizabeth's life, here are questions to help us with the intersection of scripture and her testimony. What does Elizabeth teach us?

Reflect: What priorities need to be cast aside while keeping the eyes fixed on Jesus? What does it take to be a follower of Christ?

Act: Are there justice-minded priorities that are being overlooked in the community you serve?

DAY #9 "Mrs. Nancy Rose"
Dates of service: 1871 – 1904
New York

M rs. Nancy Rose's uncle was the first keeper at Stony Point Light Station in New York in 1825. In 1852, he was followed by Mrs. Nancy Rose's husband, who died suddenly in 1871. Mrs. Nancy Rose took over all the keeper's duties, from trimming the lights, polishing the metal and glass, replenishing the lamps with oil at midnight, and keeping the fog bell running year-round. When the fog bell was moved closer to the water in 1880, Mrs. Nancy Rose had to walk up and down the hill when the fog rolled in over the Hudson River. In 1902, a red lens was put on top of the bell tower near the water, which had to be trimmed every night. Mrs. Nancy Rose took pride in keeping clean the six-room cottage she stayed in with her two children. Mrs. Nancy Rose died in 1904.

First Observations: What surprised you about her life?

Scripture to reflect on: Romans 16:13 "Rufus' mother "
"Salute Rufus chosen in the Lord, and his mother and mine." KJV

The letter of Paul to the Romans was addressing the Christian community in Rome. This appeal letter motivated the believers to spread the gospel to the western part of the Roman Empire. It was an encouragement to believers to focus on Jesus' death and resurrection. As we read this scripture and reflect on Nancy's life, here are questions to help us with the intersection of scripture and her testimony. What does Nancy teach us?

Reflect: What does Rufus' mother represent to the Christian community in Rome? What might she represent to the Suffragette movement?

<u>Act</u>: What or whom can you draw on to avoid fear, panic, and despondency in times of trauma?

DAY #10 "Mrs. Margaret Campbell & Mrs. Caroline Riddle"
Dates of service: 1869 – 1924
Louisiana

M rs. Mary Campbell became keeper of the New Canal Lighthouse in New Orleans, Louisiana, upon the death of her husband, Augustus Campbell, in 1869. She performed her daily duties of polishing the fifth order Fresnel lens, which replaced the nine oil lamps set in 14-inch reflectors. She maintained the fog bell in good working condition, until 1893.

Mrs. Caroline Riddle took over the duties from 1893 until 1924. During her time as keeper, more renovations and additions were made to the lighthouse. In 1901, a covered path was built to connect the bell tower to the lighthouse. In 1909, an oil storage shack was added. She would also row to the middle of the lake to rescue stranded fishermen, pilots, whoever needed to be rescued from many storms or shipwrecks.

First Observations: What surprised you about their lives?

Scripture to reflect on: John 4: 6 – 10 "Woman at the well"
"Now Jacob's well was there. Jesus, therefore, being wearied with his journey, sat thus on the well: and it was about the sixth hour. There cometh a woman of Samaria to draw water: Jesus saith unto her, "Give me to drink." (For his disciples were gone away unto the city to buy meat.) Then saith the woman of Samaria unto him," How is it that thou, being a Jew, askest drink of me, which am a woman of Samaria? for the Jews have no dealings with the Samaritans." Jesus answered and said unto her, "If thou knewest the gift of God, and who it is that saith to thee, Give me to drink; thou wouldest have asked of him, and he would have given thee living water."" KJV

In the gospel of John, we are reminded of the creation story, which is a fundamental anchor to the new story shared by the author. The number seven which represents completeness in Judaism, is one that is often referred to in this gospel. Jesus' public ministry is presented in seven parts and the emphasis on seven miracles Jesus performed. The apostle John is referred to as the youngest of the apostles, and whose brother James was also an apostle. They were both fishermen with their father. As we read this scripture and reflect on Margaret's and Caroline's lives, here are questions to help us with the intersection of scripture and their testimonies. What do Margaret and Caroline teach us?

Reflect: What cross-cultural barriers did Jesus break at the well? How does the woman at the well spark sentiments of perseverance in your heart?

Act: How can sacred space be made accessible to those who are being silenced in the community?

DAY #11 "Mrs. Barbara Mabrity"
Dates of service: 1832 – 1862
Florida

Mrs. Barbara Mabrity was her husband's assistant at the Key West Light Station in Florida when he was appointed keeper in 1825. When he died of yellow fever in 1832, Mrs. Barbara Mabrity took over his duties of attending to 15 whale oil fueled lamps and 15 reflectors. Her daily routine included climbing the narrow spiraling staircase to the lantern room and lighting the 15 lamps at nightfall, which were extinguished, cleaned, and polished in the mornings. Mrs. Barbara Mabrity was also raising six children. The family survived four hurricanes. At the time of the 1846 Havana hurricane, which destroyed the lighthouse, only one child was at the home with Mrs. Barbara Mabrity. They both survived. A temporary beacon was installed, which she managed. She continued to work for 16 years in a prefabricated wooden story home. In 1848 a second lighthouse was built on higher ground. It stood 15 feet above sea level. In the late 1850's, Mrs. Barbara Mabrity was assigned an assistant, whom she welcomed, given that additional duties had been tasked with the newly installed buoys around the island. During the Civil War, Mrs. Mabrity was required to oversee the new keeper's quarters, the larger lighthouse, and all the added buildings. In 1858, a third order Fresnel lens with a hydraulic lamp and three circular wicks was installed, which reduced the daily tasks of polishing, cleaning, and repairing reflectors and lenses. One night in 1859, a steamer ran ashore because both Mrs. Barbara Mabrity and her assistant were asleep during their nightly watch. In 1862, Mrs. Barbara Mabrity was accused of being too vocal about her political support to the South and was removed of her duties. Her descendants kept the lighthouse functioning until it was automated in 1915.

First Observations: What surprised you about her life?

Scripture: Matthew 26: 6 – 7 "Woman anoints Jesus"
"Now when Jesus was in Bethany, in the house of Simon the leper, there came unto him a woman having an alabaster box of very precious ointment, and poured it on his head, as he sat at meat." KJV

In the Gospel of Matthew, we are shown that God's promises to Israel had been upheld, through the coming of Jesus, God's promised Messiah. The apostle Matthew was born in Palestine and was a strong believer in the mission of Jesus. His ministry took him to serve in the East, towards Persia, away from his comfort zone. The apostle Matthew gave his heart and mind in service to The Lord. In this scripture passage, Jesus was being anointed in preparation for his upcoming death. As we read this scripture and reflect on Barbara's life, here are questions to help us with the intersection of scripture and her testimony. What does Barbara teach us?

Reflect: What spiritual practices are we being reminded of in this scripture?

Act: Who has advocated on your behalf in times of turmoil?

DAY #12 "Mrs. Fannie Mae Salter"
Dates of service: 1925 – 1947
Maryland

Mrs. Fannie Mae Salter was the last civilian woman lighthouse keeper appointed in the United States. In 1925, she was appointed keeper of Turkey Point Lighthouse in Maryland, by President Calvin Coolidge, after her husband's death. Mrs. Fannie Mae Salter retired after 22 years of service once the lighthouse became automated in 1947. During her time of service at Turkey Point, the US Coast Guard installed a radio-telephone, which Mrs. Fannie Mae learned to operate from a manual. She made regular reports of weather conditions to navigation authorities. The radio-telephone became her lifeline in the winter when snow kept her stranded. Up until electricity was installed in 1943 at the lighthouse, Mrs. Fannie Mae was going up and down the lighthouse tower, up to five times a day to carry oil, clean the lens, clean the lantern floor, do some interior and exterior painting, pump water, and other necessary chores to maintain the running of the lighthouse and the caretaker's home. The oil lamps were kept as "back up" lamps in case the electricity was interrupted.

First Observations: What surprised you about her life?

Scripture to reflect on: Matthew 9: 20 – 22 "Hemorrhaging Woman"
"And, behold, a woman, which was diseased with an issue of blood twelve years, came behind him, and touched the hem of his garment: For she said within herself, "If I may but touch his garment, I shall be whole." But Jesus turned him about, and when he saw her, he said, "Daughter, be of good comfort; thy faith hath made thee whole." And the woman was made whole from that hour." KJV

In the Gospel of Matthew, we are shown that God's promises to Israel had been upheld, through the coming of Jesus, God's promised Messiah. The apostle Matthew was born in Palestine and was a strong believer in the mission of Jesus. His ministry took him to serve in the East, towards Persia, away from his comfort zone. Matthew gave his heart and mind in service to The Lord. In this scripture passage, Jesus demonstrated compassion, grace, restoration, humanity, and dignity.

As we read this scripture and reflect on Fannie Mae's life, here are questions to help us with the intersection of scripture and her testimony. What does Fannie Mae teach us?

Reflect: What surprises you about the boldness of the woman in this scripture passage? Did the woman believe in complete healing?

Act: How might acts of individual and corporate restoration be shown locally and globally?

Epilogue

D r. Lynn Domina shares in her book entitled *Devotions from HerStory: 31 Days with women of faith*" even nameless women can be honored, and their trust, faith, and actions can inspire us even when we don't know exactly who they are" (p.VIII)

I am grateful to God's nudging and accompaniment to have brought light to these 15 women lighthouse keepers, whose stories are incomplete and yet have been told in a unique way, in this devotional. I have attempted to give voice to voiceless women of the 19th and 20th century, who dedicated their lives and well-being, to serve others. They sustained life.

I am grateful to the leadership at International Ministries, to have granted me a time of sabbatical in 2021, to do the necessary research and writing which produced *Beacons of Hope*.

I hold in deep gratitude, the special village of family and close friends who accompanied me in prayer, sacred space, songs, and nourishment. You made all this possible.

My sincere thanks to the Heidi Lynn Fuller Ministry Support Fund for their generous financial support to cover my travel expenses.

This work is meant to be part of a beginning conversation about transformation, gender equity, dignity, and servant-leadership roles women have held for many centuries, whether publicly recognized and affirmed or in the shadows. The stories need to be unearthed and shared. From the beginning of time, women have been prophets, healers, counselors, judges, tent makers, and more. Women appear in the Bible with names, like "Miriam, Esther, Sarah, Deborah, Lydia, Ruth, Mary, ..." and without names but defined by their function, ailment, or genealogy, like "Pharaoh's daughter, the Phoenician Woman, Rufus' mother, the Woman at the well, the Woman with the issue of blood..." How well do we know their stories?

In a way the women lighthouse keepers have remained unknown to the multitude of strangers they saved and served; hence the parallel I chose to make with the scripture references of the unnamed women of the Bible. We don't fully know all the women keepers of lighthouses in the United States. The gender inequity is flagrant, as many were paid much less than their male counterparts. Some had to depend on the community to advocate on their behalf to the US Lighthouse Establishment for them to receive their salary. They stayed the course and provided safe passage to all ships in the bays, rivers, shores they guarded. If these vessels were in danger, the keepers did not hesitate to attempt to rescue the sailors. Human life was to be honored.

As I think of all these women of the 19th and 20th century, I find myself reflecting on another group of women who stepped out in faith alongside their spouses and accepted the charge to serve. These are the spouses of missionaries who crossed the seas to bring God's good news to other countries.

I think of Rev. Lott Carey's second wife, Nancy Cary, who left her home in Richmond (Virginia) to accompany her husband who felt called to share the Gospel in West Africa. She died in 1821 on the way to Liberia. Were her last seven words captured by anyone?

I also think of Hannah Liele, wife of George Liele, both freed slaves from Georgia en route to serve in Jamaica. Hannah served alongside her husband and ministered to many in slave quarters on plantations. Do we know her favorite scripture passages?

Lastly, I think of Phyllis George, who was part Creek Indian, and was married to David George in the mid 1770's. They escaped the atrocities of slavery and headed to Shelburne, Nova Scotia, where David George planted a church, and became a leader of the Baptist congregations of the African American Loyalists. Nothing is known about Phyllis' ministry, nor her life in Nova Scotia. Did she develop strong connections with other local women? Or did she stay to herself, because of her heritage?

I trust that mentioning these names today will be a motivator to seek "the more" of these heroic women's footprints on earth. By God's grace, may you continue to be inspired to speak, and may we seek, find, and sustain hope.

Bibliography

Clifford, Mary Louise and Candace, *Mind the Light, Katie: The history of thirty-three female lighthouse keepers*. Waltham, MA: Cypress Communications, 2006

Clifford, Mary Louise and Candace, *Women Who Kept the Lights: An illustrated history of female lighthouse keepers*. Waltham, MA: Cypress Communications 2013

Discavage, Michelle, *Unnamed Women of the Bible: Lessons of value, belonging and worth*. CreateSpace Independent Publishing Platform, 1st edition (May 24, 2016)

Domina, Lynn, *Devotions from Herstory: 31 Days with women of faith*. King of Prussia, PA: Judson Press 2019

The Bible, *King James Version*

CPSIA information can be obtained
at www.ICGtesting.com
Printed in the USA
BVHW090922090222
628493BV00017B/434